B6

English G 21

Klassenarbeitstrainer

für Schülerinnen und Schüler

Lösungen und Lerntipps

Cornelsen

Lösungen A

LISTENING

01 1 A radio phone-in – today's topic: How did you meet your partner?

Presenter Good morning and a very warm welcome to the show! Today we're going to be talking about the wonderful topic of "love". We want to know: where did you meet your husband, wife, boyfriend or girlfriend? So call in and tell us the story of the love of your life!

Great, we have our first caller. Good morning, Lisa. We're very excited to hear your story. Where did you meet your man?

Lisa Oh, hi. Good morning, John. Well, I think my story is very romantic. It was the day before my 20th birthday. It was a pretty stressful day because I'd planned a big party but I hadn't bought anything for it yet. So after work I went straight to the supermarket and threw everything into a shopping basket. But guess what happened when I was at the cash desk and wanted to pay? I realized that I didn't have any money with me! I was so embarrassed! You know, this all happened 25 years ago when credit cards weren't very common yet … I had everything packed in my bags already and the queue behind me was getting longer and longer. I didn't have the time to leave my shopping there and come back because I had to go straight to my evening classes. And then suddenly, the young man behind me offered to pay for my shopping. It was so lovely of him! And he didn't ask for anything from me in return, he just said he was sure I would pay him back later. So he gave me his business card with his address on it and wrote his bank details on it. That was all. I was so lucky! I took my shopping and went to my classes. The next morning I bought a bottle of wine and went to the young man's home. I gave him the money and invited him to my birthday party. We had a wonderful evening and started dating. Well, yes, what can I say? We fell in love and got married three years later. We've been married ever since, have three wonderful children and, yes, of course, we sometimes fight, but we're still very happy. So, there you have it – that's my story!

Presenter What a wonderful and romantic story, Lisa! Thank you for sharing it with us.

Lerntipp **Notizen machen während des Anhörens**

Finde heraus, welche Methode des Mitschreibens für dich am besten passt. Du kannst mit einer Mindmap arbeiten oder Stichworte aufschreiben. Auf jeden Fall solltest du Daten (Wochentage, Jahr, ...) oder Zahlen (Preise, ...), die in einem Text vorkommen, für dich schriftlich festhalten.

a)

1 Lisa talks about	a) her birthday and the day before.	✔
	b) her 20th birthday.	
	c) a man in her evening classes.	
	d) her birthday presents.	

2 The young man	a) used his credit card.	
	b) didn't want to have the money back.	
	c) was standing behind Lisa.	✔
	d) wanted to go to Lisa's party.	

3 Lisa and the young man	a) drank a bottle of French wine together.	
	b) started going out after her party.	✔
	c) want to get married soon.	
	d) want to have at least three children.	

4 After Lisa's story, the reporter says that	a) another person is going to tell their story.	
	b) there is a break now.	
	c) he liked the story.	✔
	d) they are going to play a love song.	

02 *Presenter* And now we have Nick on the line. Hello, Nick. You have a bit of a heartbreaking story for us, right?

Nick Yes, mm, hi. I wanted to tell the story about my first love.

Presenter OK, great, go on then.

Nick Well, yeah. It was the beginning of year ten at school. There was a new girl in our class. She was from London and she was pretty! You know, I was at school in Bristol, and we thought she was so cool! All the boys in my class fancied her and we did many really stupid things to get her to notice us. You know, all that teenage stuff like writing letters, recording cassettes with the latest love songs, acting all cool and trying to look like we didn't care about anything when really we were like jelly inside! You know, stupid teenage stuff. To be honest, I never thought I'd have a chance with her because, well, I'm pretty average-looking. But I was lucky because one weekend I went to a course on how to apply for jobs and to my surprise she was there as well. I was impressed because I hadn't thought she was interested in stuff like that ... But, anyway, we had a lot of fun together. We didn't know anyone else on the course so we worked as a pair on all the tasks for the whole day. Afterwards we went out for a drink. We had a great evening and other dates followed, you know. That was the beginning of a wonderful love story. We were together for four years before we broke up. That was ten years ago now. She got married since then, as did I, but we still have contact by email.

Presenter Thanks, Nick. That one was a little sad somehow, but still a great story, thank you. Hope your wife isn't jealous ...

Nick No, there's no need for that!

Presenter Well, then, thanks for calling! – And now, anybody else wanting to tell the listeners their romantic story? Call us! We're back after some music to chat with the next caller.

b)

1 in London
2 wrote letters, recorded cassettes with love songs, tried to look cool
3 on a course
4 because they didn't know the others
5 four years
6 they are in contact by email

03 *Presenter* Hi everyone and welcome back. We're talking about great love stories today. So, Anna has a wonderful multicultural story for us. Hi Anna, share it with us!

Anna Hi John. Well, I got to know my boyfriend when my cousin got married two months ago. My cousin lives in Germany, and her boyfriend – or husband – is from England. They had their party in a nice restaurant outside Harrogate. Of course, there were also lots of Germans there, and they wanted to make sure the guests all chatted with each other, so they placed German and English people next to each other so that never two neighbours were from the same country. A lot of the Germans spoke really good English but others didn't at all. A boy about my age, I'm 17, was sitting next to me. He was very sweet but we had some trouble talking to each other because, well, he didn't really speak English and, umm, my German isn't very good either. So, as you can imagine, at first it was pretty hard and we just sat there for ages! But he seemed really nice, so I tried really hard to find a topic that we could talk about. After a while we got onto films and that was the ice breaker! Not that we could suddenly talk to each other perfectly or anything, but it was way better than before. We found we liked the same kinds of films and had the same sense of humour, so we made a date to go to the cinema the next day. And I swear – we had the best time ever! I've never had as much fun as I did that evening. It was such a great date, and we spent loads of time together the week he was in England. I really felt like we were falling in love by the end of the week.

Presenter And then what happened?

Anna Yeah, well then he had to go back to Germany because he's training to be a chef. I still go to college here in England but I'm finishing in the summer. After that I want to go to Germany and learn his language. I just want to be near him! And I think that's what he wants too. I don't know how the whole thing is going to turn out, but I hope we'll end up as a happy family.

Presenter Oh, wow, Anna, very romantic. Thank you! We all wish you lots of luck!

c)

1 Anna got to know her boyfriend two months ago at her cousin's wedding.

2 Her cousin is from Germany, and her husband is from England.

3 Anna sat next to a German boy.

4 The German boy didn't speak English very well.

5 Their conversation got better when they started to talk about films.

6 On the day after the wedding party they went to see a film together.

7 When Anna has finished college, she wants to go to Germany.

04 ***Presenter*** Right, the next caller is on the line: Leo. He's only 18 but already completely in love. So, hi Leo. Where did you meet your lovely lady?

Leo Hi John, I'm so excited to be on the radio! OK, so here's my story: a while ago I started going to dancing classes at a local club with a friend of mine. I know that sounds pretty stupid, but my mate is such a good dancer and he told me I needed to work on my moves a bit, as girls really like a good dancer. We were really lucky, because the class had way more girls than boys in it, so it was easy to find a dance partner – yeah, it was pretty cool to be able to pick and choose! Anyway, so I danced – or well, I tried to dance – with different girls, but it is way harder than it looks on TV, I can tell you! I couldn't remember all the steps and I kept messing up, treading on the girls' toes and all that. Pretty embarrassing ... Anyway, there was one really sweet girl there, but I didn't get to talk to her much because I had to concentrate on the dance steps, and at the end of the class she disappeared so I never got to chat her up. Actually, I think I was just happy it was the end of the class by that point! I never wanted to go back again, but I couldn't get this girl out of my head, so I ended up going again the next week. And that time I asked her on a date at the end of the class! That was six months ago, and now we are completely in love but I haven't tried to dance since then! She really wants me to go to the dance class with her again and it's her birthday coming up next week, so I was thinking I might take her there as a surprise. I'll see ...

Presenter Great idea! Be brave, young man, and surprise her! Thanks for your story and say hello to your girlfriend. You can practise dancing to the next song, Leo. Well, I hope all you listeners are feeling romantic too. That's the end of our phone-in. Thanks for sharing all your stories! Next up, we're talking about the latest films coming out at the cinema. Don't miss it!

d)

	right	wrong
1 Leo had invited a friend to a dancing club.		✔
2 There were more boys than girls.		✔
3 Leo talked a lot to the nice girl.		✔
4 Leo had some problems with dancing.	✔	
5 Perhaps Leo will go to the classes again.	✔	

e)

Mögliche Lösungen:

1 A friend had invited Leo to a dancing club.

2 There were more girls than boys.

3 Leo didn't talk to the girl a lot because he had to concentrate on the steps.

05 2 At the café

Catherine Um, excuse me. Is this seat taken or do you mind if I sit at your table?

Jonathan Oh no, of course not. Sit down, please.

Catherine Thank you. Could I have a look through the job advertisements in your newspaper? Or were you still going to read it?

Jonathan No sure, take it. What job are you looking for? Oh, sorry: I'm Jonathan.

Catherine Hi Jonathan, I'm Catherine. Nice to meet you. Oh, I'm just looking for a part-time job – anything really. To make a bit of extra money, you know.

Jonathan Oh, yeah, I know what you mean. What have you done so far?

Catherine Well, I've just finished school, but my results are only average. I really want to go to art school but I have to hand in some examples of my artwork to get a place at the college. So I need to work on my paintings and drawings for the next few months. And I need equipment, which is really, really expensive. So that's why I need the job. What about you?

Jonathan I finished school last year and at the moment I'm training to be a mechanic in a little garage near here.

Catherine Really? That's cool. And do you like your job? How did you get into mechanics?

Jonathan Yeah, I love the job. I'm really happy to have it as well, because it's a good chance to prepare for technical college. It's a lot of work every day but I'm learning lots of things there. I already know a lot about cars and now I can repair my father's car, which is pretty cool. I want to have a car of my own so I need to save money every week for that. But I'm not saving that much, because I also want to have a life, you know? Go out with friends, party, all that kind of stuff. So, I really know what you are talking about with your art school and the job. Life's really expensive. Do you still live with your parents?

Catherine Yeah, I do. That makes things a bit easier.

Jonathan So, is this going to be your first job then or have you had another job before?

Catherine No, it isn't. I worked as a waitress in a little café before. But it was nowhere near as busy as this one and it was a bit boring working there, and after six months I needed a change. After that I worked in a mobile phone shop but that wasn't for me. I like texting my mates and calling people on my mobile but that's not all I'm interested in.

Jonathan So what job are you looking for now?

Catherine Yeah, well, that's exactly the problem: I don't know where to look for a job. It's so hard and I'm getting really down about it. Do you have any suggestions?

→

Jonathan	Umm, let me think. Why don't you try a supermarket or a bookshop? You could pop in directly and ask if they need help. Or maybe in a hospital? Or, hey, a friend of mine works in a travel agency, and she says it's really fun.
Catherine	That sounds great! Thanks for the ideas. I think I'll definitely try the travel agencies.
Jonathan	Cool. Oh, sorry I've really got to get back to work, my break's over. It was nice talking to you though. And well, maybe we could meet up again sometime?
Catherine	Sure, I'd like that. Then I can tell you all about my brilliant career! You can call me if you like. I'll give you my number. It's 07894 …

a)

A 8, B 1, C 3, D 4, E 2, F 5, G 7, H 6

b)

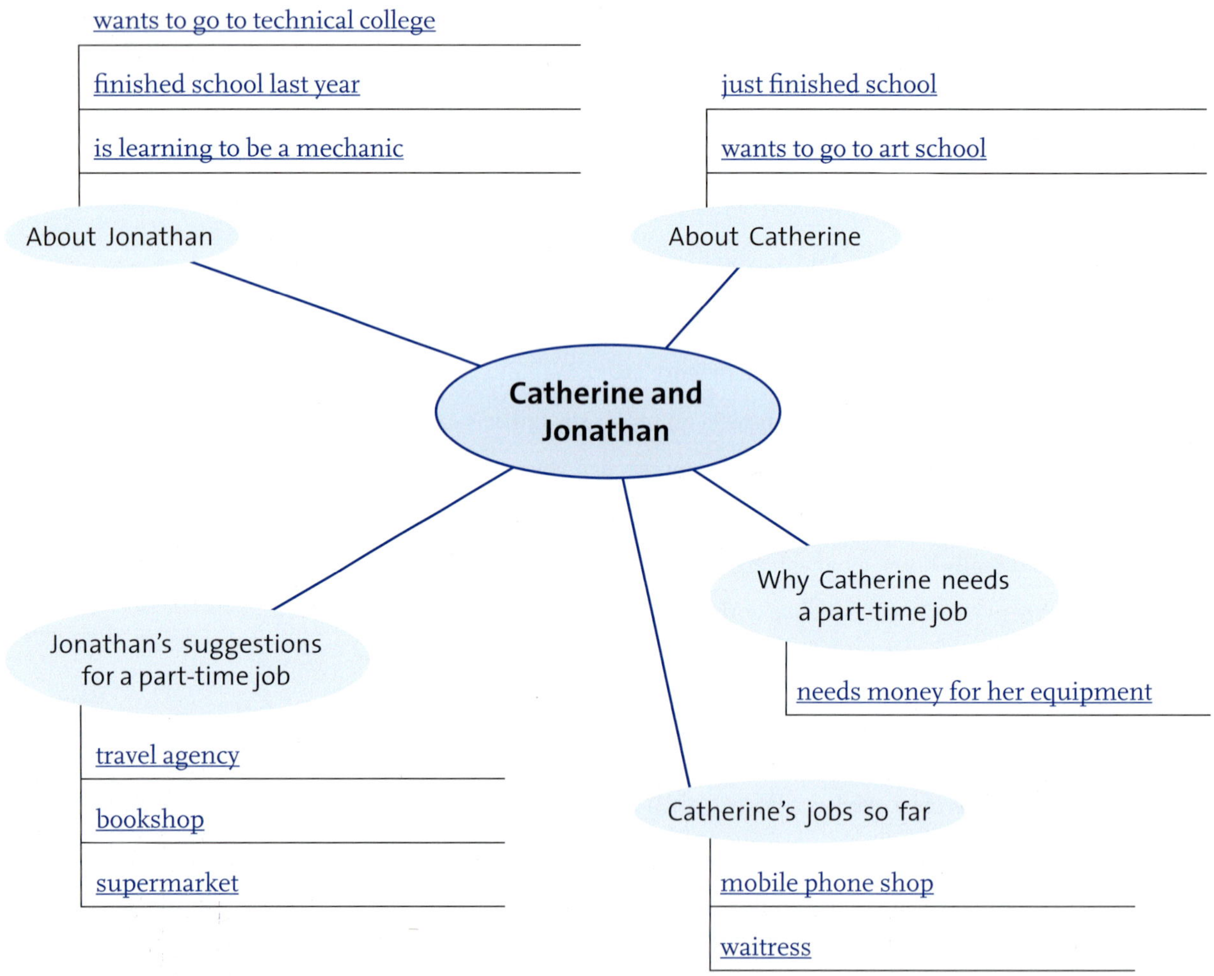

LANGUAGE

1 WORDS Me and my friends

I have many friends, boys and girls. Their appearance is different. Most of them are quite thin, some have straight hair, only three of them have curly hair. Some of the girls are really good-looking and attractive.
I don't like arrogant people, so of course all of them are really charming.
Ah, you want to know some things about me too? Well, I think I'm a lovable person with a good sense of humour. I don't like working so much so some people say that I'm lazy. But I laugh a lot and I always talk to people in a friendly way. Normally I'm not nervous because I have a lot of confidence in what I'm doing. Perhaps I should also mention that I like to flirt with the girls.

Lösung für die blue boxes: loyal

2 GRAMMAR My friends and their hobbies

Mara, one of my friends, loves taking photos. She always carries her camera around. She doesn't take any photos of people, she always takes photos of nature. Here you can see her. She is taking a photo of a flower.
Susan loves languages. At the moment she is learning Dutch. She speaks English, Spanish and Italian.
She doesn't speak Portuguese but she also wants to learn German.
Here you can see Philip, Chris and Ava. They don't like watching TV, in fact one of them even hates it.
Sometimes they watch a film at the cinema. In this photo they are playing one of their many board games.

3 GRAMMAR REVISION + A social day for Mike and his friends

a)

"We had decided to join the 'Community Day' long before the actual day. We simply wanted to do something for our town. And we thought it would be fun working together. It was our job to clean places inside and outside town. We started at the station where we didn't find a lot of rubbish. We were more successful when we went to the small river near our town. We found many different things: a lot of rubbish like paper, plastic and glasses, of course, but also a mobile phone, a watch and an old school-bag. After we had taken away all the rubbish, we tried to find the owner of the mobile phone. As we weren't successful in finding him or her, we took it to the lost property office. In the evening we were invited to an Italian restaurant by the mayor of our town."

b)

had decided, had taken
I use the past perfect when I want to show that something had happened before another action in the past.
Mögliche Lösungen:

1 After I had done my homework, I watched a film.
2 Pete went to France when he had passed his exam.
3 They had bought their tickets before they went to the cinema.

Lerntipp **Simple past und past perfect – unregelmäßige Verben**

- Für die Bildung dieser zwei Zeiten musst du sicher in den unregelmäßigen Verben sein.
- Noch einmal zur Erinnerung: Das **simple past** wird mit der 2. Form und das **past perfect** wird mit **had** plus der 3. Form des Verbs gebildet.
- Wiederhole daher die unregelmäßigen Verben. Du findest sie in deinem Englischbuch auf S. 224–225.

MEDIATION

Ein Freund, ein guter Freund

Mögliche Lösungen:

1 The topic of the festival is "good friends". The film should be about a friend who is always there for you and helps you in difficult situations. In the film, you can show a situation where your friend has problems with his parents and how you can help him or her. Another idea is that you make a film about problems at school, e.g. when you are bullied. (4P)

2 You can send in a complete short film or an idea for a film or a cartoon. (3P)

3 You have to send it in by February 1st, the film mustn't be longer than four minutes and you mustn't be older than 14. (3P)

4 There are teenagers and adults in the jury. The winning film will be shown at the national film festival in October. The winner of the second place will get 150 euros as a price, the winner of the third place will get 100 euros. (4P)

WRITING

How I got to know ...

Two years ago my marks for Maths became very bad. So my parents sent me to evening classes especially for Maths. I didn't want to go there but I had to. (3P)

And that's where I met Pete. He was a student at the evening classes too. I liked him from the first moment. (3P) He was in the same situation as me. But he really wanted to become better. I liked him for this. It helped me with my Maths. (4P) We both started to believe in ourselves, we even learned Maths together. (2P)

And with the help of the young teacher we started to like Maths and became better within a short period of time. Pete and I became very good friends and we still are today. (4P)

READING

YFC – Young Film Competition

a)

		Yes – there is an answer in the text	No – sorry, no answer in the text
1	Is it an international competition?	✔	
2	Is any topic allowed?	✔	
3	Can the three of us work together on one idea?		✔
4	At what age can we take part?	✔	
5	How many pages do we have to hand in?		✔
6	Can we hand in two different ideas?		✔
7	Do we get any help from YFC?	✔	
8	Will every film be produced?	✔	
9	Will other people have the chance to watch the films?	✔	
10	How many people took part in the last few years?		✔
11	What are the prizes?		✔
12	How can we find out more about the film festival?	✔	

b)

Mögliche Lösungen:

1 No, it isn't. It's only for young Canadian people.

2 No, the topics should be based on the following three subjects: relationship, bullying or the environment.

4 You can take part if you are between 12 and 22 years old.

7 Yes, you get help from the website. When your film is produced, you get help from professional film producers.

8 Yes, there will be a festival for the public in June.

9 No, only the ten best film ideas will be produced.

12 You can write a mail to yfc@yfcfestival-film.com.

LANGUAGE

1 WORDS About films

1 Many people read a review about the film before they go to the cinema.

2 Sometimes films are different from the books that they are based on.

3 Susan likes films with friendship and love, she likes romantic films.

4 I love watching films directed by James Cameron.

5 People who are interested in history like films that are set in previous centuries.

6 Action movies are very cool, I like the special effects.

7 The Oscar is the most famous film award.

8 We can have a bet on whether you'll like the film. Believe me: you'll love it.

9 Pete wanted to see this new film that stars Brad Pitt.

10 Unfortunately, he broke his leg, so he couldn't go to the cinema.

2 WORDS Getting by in English

1 Elly dumped/broke up with her boyfriend.

2 I didn't catch your name.

3 Ann is very arrogant unlike her brother Adam who is very charming.

4 I am not going to the party either.

3 GRAMMAR A survey on young people

Mögliche Lösungen:

1 No, she doesn't. She does her homework on Monday, Tuesday and Wednesday.

2 Linn usually meets her friends at the weekend.

3 Dave plays computer games twice a week.

4 Joe often does sports.

5 Joe and Dave never learn German vocabulary.

6 No, he doesn't. He helps his parents on Saturday.

7 Dave and Linn both always do their homework on Monday.

4 GRAMMAR REVISION + What will be in the future?

Interviewer We now have the chance to talk to one of our young film-makers here ... So, Joanna, thank you for the exciting film about the two friends. Now, let's talk a bit about your future. What can you tell us about it?

Joanna Well, I hope I will have the chance to make many more films in the future, so that I will be able to learn more about film-making. I hope I will go to a film academy in the near future.

Interviewer We will be glad to see more of your films. I'm sure you will make other exciting films and will be able to go to the film acadamy. Are there any topics you are especially interested in and are there others you are not interested in, Joanna?

Joanna Well, I can definitely say I will not make any detective stories because I'm not interested in crime stories. I suppose I will go on making films about relationships, I think this is something people are always interested in.

Interviewer Many people will be happy to hear about your plans for more films. I'm sure you will become famous.

Joanna Thanks very much. I hope so too.

Interviewer Thank you and goodbye.

5 GRAMMAR REVISION + My ideas for the film

I had the idea for "Her Eyes" when I was in the swimming pool last summer. Suddenly I saw this girl who wasn't particularly pretty, but her eyes were special. But I didn't talk to her. After I had left the swimming pool, I still thought about her eyes and started making up a love story. First I didn't write down anything, I just thought of ideas. But because I hadn't written down my ideas, I soon forgot them. So I decided to write them on small pieces of paper. That was a really good idea. After about three weeks I had collected all my ideas and I then wrote down everything. The film was produced this year in February.

Lerntipp Verwendung des past perfect

- Überlege noch einmal, warum an den drei Stellen in der obenstehenden Aufgabe das **past perfect** verwendet werden muss.
- Bilde weitere Sätze, in denen man **past perfect** verwenden muss.
- So kannst du dir am einfachsten darüber klar werden, wie es verwendet wird.

6 GRAMMAR REVISION + A backstage meeting

Mögliche Lösungen:

At what age did you decide to become an actor?

Did you have difficult years before you became a star?

Do you still like your job?

What are your plans for the future?

Do you already know the title of your next film?

What would you advise a person who wants to become an actor?

Lerntipp Bildung von Fragen

- Das Grammar File 2 auf S. 153 in deinem Englischbuch listet verschiedene Möglichkeiten der Fragebildung auf.
- Nutze es, wann immer du Fragen bilden willst (außer natürlich bei Klassenarbeiten in der Schule!).
- Du kannst dir selbst weitere solche Aufgaben stellen: Überlege dir eine Person (aus dem Freundeskreis, berühmte Stars oder Politiker) und überlege dir Fragen, die du dieser Person stellen möchtest.
- Überprüfe deine Fragen anhand des Lösungsvorschlags zu dieser Aufgabe und des Grammar File 2.
- Hole dir beim Überprüfen auch immer mal wieder Hilfe von deinem Lehrer/deiner Lehrerin oder einer anderen Person, die gut Englisch spricht.

MEDIATION

Almanya – Willkommen in Deutschland

Mögliche Lösung:

Six-year-old Cenk Yilmaz doesn't know if he is German or Turkish. (1P) His cousin Canan tells him his grandfather's story. (1P) His grandfather Hüseyin came to Germany as a Turkish worker in the 1960s. Later the whole family came to Germany, too. (2P) Canan talks about their life in Germany and about their dreams and the many problems they had in the foreign country. (3P) One evening the grandfather has a surprise for the whole family. He has bought a house in Turkey for their holidays. (2P) The whole family travels to Turkey. (1P) During the journey they remember things from the past. (1P)

In the end, something surprising happens during their journey and Cenk gets a very special job. (2P)

SPEAKING

06 An interview with a young film-maker

Luke Let's talk about the beginning of your film career. How did you get the idea of making a film when you were only 17?

Neil Well, when I was a child I loved going to the cinema with my dad. And then we did a project about films at school where we even produced some short scenes. I think that was the beginning.

Luke And then at 15 you started with "My Wave". It's a film about young people's lives, their happy moments, but also about their sad moments with a lot of problems. Where did you get the inspiration for the film from?

Neil Hm, some parts describe moments from my own life, but for many others parts I got the inspiration from people I watched, also from my friends of course.

Luke Did you want to give a message to the audience of your film?

Neil When I made the film, I didn't think about messages. But today I'm sure that my film does give a message to young people. It's quite easy really: don't give up even if you face a lot of problems, try to see things positively and talk about your problems.

Luke You also played a role in your film. How did you do that? It was probably very difficult to direct the film and to act at the same time.

Neil It definitely was difficult, sometimes I had problems managing. But I think it is important to understand the two different roles and to see them as two separate jobs. And, of course, you have to be honest with yourself and your own acting.

Luke What did a normal day look like for you?

Neil The days of the production were really hard work because we worked for 10 sometimes even 12 hours a day and we did this 6 days a week.

Luke This doesn't sound romantic at all. Were there moments when you thought, 'oh I wish I hadn't started with this film'?

Neil Oh no, I loved this work too much to have thoughts like that although it was hard work.

Luke Are you working on another film at the moment?

Neil No, I'm not, I'm having a break right now. I need time to think about further projects.

Luke Sounds as if you already have ideas for the future. Will you make another film?

Neil Definitely yes, I will.

Luke Can you tell us about your plans?

→

Neil I'd like to make a film about bullying at school. But this needs a lot of research before I can start working on the film.

Luke Well that just leaves us to wish you all the best for your future work. And – we are looking forward to more of your films. Thank you for the interview.

Neil You're welcome.

Now you

Mögliche Lösung:

You Let's talk about the making of your film "Old Mrs Creek's dog". How did you get the idea for this film? (2P)

Your partner This is a funny story. My grandmother has a dog and she doesn't talk to many people during the day but to her dog. This is a bit strange but she is very happy and I thought this could make a funny film.

You That's really interesting. What is the film about? Can you tell us a bit about the content? (3P)

Your partner As the title says, it's about an old woman and her dog. It shows the normal day of an old lady who lives alone in a small house and she only speaks to her dog. It is about the relationship between them.

You Making the film must have been funny. Can you tell us a bit about it? (2P)

Your partner Yes, sure. The grandmother is my own grandmother and she liked it very much. She loved being the main actor in the film. And the dog is her own dog. This was rather difficult because the dog often didn't do what we wanted him to do.

You Yes, I see what you mean. Are there only those two characters in the film? (1P)

Your partner Yes, it's only granny and her dog.

You OK. Another thing I would like to ask you: What about your future? Do you already have any plans for the future? (3P)

Your partner Well, I'm only 12 years old so I don't have real plans for the future. At the moment it's only school, school, school. But I love animals very much, maybe I'll become a vet some day.

You OK. Good luck for your future and thank you for your funny film! Bye. (2P)

Your partner Thank you. Bye.

Lerntipp **So kannst du Speaking üben**

Du kannst den Dialog auch noch einmal mit dem anderen Filmplakat üben.
Wenn du möchtest, können du und dein Partner/deine Partnerin bei einem weiteren Durchgang auch die Rollen tauschen.

READING

1 Teenagers and the media

a)

Mögliche Lösungen:

1 Name two things about teenagers and TV.	– they (many of them) say they can do without it more than without their mobile – they watch more TV than ever		
2 Give the percentage of children from lower classes who don't have access to the internet.	20 %		
3 Name two things teenagers use the internet for.	education, entertainment		
4 Write down the percentage of children who would miss their mobile, the internet and the TV this year and last year.		this year	last year
	mobile	28 %	31 %
	internet	25 %	24 %
	TV	18 %	24 %
5 Write down the number of teenagers who listen to the radio.	about half of them		
6 Name the place in the house where most children use the internet.	living room		
7 Write down percentage increase in children with a smartphone from last year to this year.	10 %		

b)

1 Not all children have internet access.

2 The survey is carried out every year.

3 More parents care about how their children use the internet.

4 Many younger children use the internet together with an adult in the room.

5 More than half of the children aged 8–11 use a mobile.

Lerntipp **Unbekannte Wörter erschließen**

- Lies dir noch einmal den Handhinweis vor dem Lesetext dieser Klassenarbeit genau durch.
- Trainiere das Erschließen unbekannter Wörter so oft es geht. Das kann im Unterricht mit einem unbekannten Text sein oder auch Zuhause, wenn du einen Text im Internet liest.

2 A do-it-yourself workshop

a)

1 Customers come to the bike workshop	a) when they are looking for a new bike.	
	b) when they have a problem with their bike.	✔
	c) when they are looking for somebody to repair their bike.	

2 Bike workshops	a) can also be found in other cities.	✔
	b) are always a big risk.	
	c) are run by people for their friends.	

3 Emma wasn't sure	a) if she really wanted a bike workshop.	
	b) if her friends would help to renovate the garage.	
	c) if she could earn enough money with the bike workshop.	✔

4 Henry	a) repairs the bikes.	
	b) thinks that people must get to know their bikes.	✔
	c) likes the atmosphere in the bike workshop.	

5 Emma is sure that	a) the bike workshop helps the environment.	✔
	b) everybody can make his or her individual bike with many different parts.	
	c) the author of the article will find the missing part he is looking for.	

6 Most of the customers	a) don't have much money.	
	b) would prefer to repair their bikes at home.	
	c) are bike fans.	✔

b)

Mögliche Lösungen:

What are the opening hours of the bike workshop?

When did you open the bike workshop?

How many customers do you have per day?

Would you like to open another bike workshop?

Do you earn enough money to live on it?

LANGUAGE

1 WORDS From the newspapers

1 Since 1970 British households have needed about 34% more energy. Use gadgets that save energy!

2 The Latest figures show that UK emissions fell by 7% in 2011.

3 Will Britain reach its targets and reduce its carbon footprint?

4 The discovery of a new medicine might help the fight against AIDS.

5 Because of the warm winter, less power was needed in Britain.

6 A Brighton high school student is proud of his new invention. Look at his solar barbecue.

7 The insulation of the town hall will cost more than expected.

8 Global warming is the most complicated environmental problem the world has to solve.

9 Greenhouse gases are mainly produced by burning fossil fuels.

10 The amount of carbon dioxide produced rose again.

2 WORDS A crossword

Across

1 power cut 7 conditions 8 gadget

Down

2 responsible 3 pretend 4 choice 5 no-no 6 bill

3 GRAMMAR REVISION + My bike is repaired

a)

Adam Have you got a new bike? Your old one is broken, isn't it?

Oliver I wasn't able to afford a new one, so I repaired my old one.

Adam I don't believe it! Did you repair it yourself?

Oliver Yes, I did. I was able to do it with the help of the bike workshop down the road.

Adam Hey, it must be new. I haven't heard of it.

Oliver Yes, it is. It's great! I went there with my broken bike. A young man showed me round and then I was allowed to use all the tools they have.

Adam What about new parts?

Oliver Ah, good question. You don't have to buy expensive new parts. They have hundreds of used parts, and you simply look for the part you need. Of course, you have to pay for it. I also had to pay for using the workshop at the end, but believe me, it was a fair price. I was able to pay it from my pocket-money.

b)

Mögliche Lösungen:

1 I'm able to go to school by bike.

2 I wasn't able to go by bike when I was four years old.

3 I'm not allowed to drive a car.

4 Last week my bike was broken so I had to go to school by bus.

5 Last week I had to repair my bike.

4 GRAMMAR REVISION + About the environmental projects

a)

	who	which	that	not necessary
1 The project were we plant trees is the project ____________ I like best.		✔	✔	✔
2 Look, there is the girl ____________ is in the same project as me.	✔		✔	
3 The head teacher is talking to the students of the project ____________ deals with the pollution of the air.		✔	✔	
4 Sue and Carmelita are the two girls ____________ I work with in my project.	✔		✔	✔
5 Alan is the one ____________ is responsible for painting the posters in his project.	✔		✔	

b)

Mögliche Lösungen:

1 Oliver is the boy who/that I got to know in my project.

2 Repairing old bikes is the project which/that I would like to choose.

3 The boy who/that rang up five minutes ago is in my project too.

WRITING

Gadgets on class trips

Our school rules say that we are not allowed to take mobile phones and MP3-players with us. (1P)

I think it is OK not to allow MP3-players. On a class trip, the whole class should be together and have fun together. When everybody just listens to his or her own music, we cannot be a team. (3P) But I don't think it is a good idea to leave our mobile phones at home. It can be very useful to have a mobile phone. On a day trip, for example, students are sometimes allowed to go somewhere in small groups. But what happens if they lose their way or if they are late? If some of them have a mobile with them, they can easily call the teacher. Maybe they are in a dangerous situation. Then they can also call the police. (4P)

I think they should change the rules and should allow the students to take their mobiles with them. Maybe it is a good idea to ban texting. (2P)

LISTENING

07 1 Talking about the environment

Host Hello and welcome back to the show all about our wonderful environment. Our listeners have called up with questions they'd like to ask and our expert Amanda Stokker is going to answer them. She's in the studio with me. Good morning Amanda.

Amanda Hi, good morning. It's great to be here.

Host It's great to have you here. We have a very interesting question from one of our listeners: Michael from Washington. He asks: "What's better for the environment: flying or driving?" So, Amanda, it's your turn now.

Amanda That is indeed an interesting question and the answer is simple: Let's say he wants to do a trip of about 300 miles. Going by car is better for the environment if you have quite a fuel-efficient, medium-sized car. Then driving produces about 104 kilograms of CO_2. Flying in a normal plane would produce about 184 kilograms of CO_2 per passenger.

Host Wow, that's a huge difference. How many passengers are in the car then?

Amanda Only one. Surprising isn't it? And, of course, it would be even better if there were more than one person in the car: if you have four people in the car, it's still only 104 kilograms of CO_2 produced in total or 26 kilograms per person. If you compare that to a flight of 300 miles: the amount of CO_2 produced for four people on the flight is 736 kilograms! So you can see, driving in this case would be an easy way to do something for the environment.

Host Yes, it would be. But what about the price of the gas for the car and the cost of flights?

Amanda As we all know, gas prices are quite high. That's what makes driving far more expensive if you're going the same distance. So flying is cheaper, and that's exactly why many people prefer flying. Yeah, and, umm, of course, flying also saves time, as we probably all know. But, if you're not travelling that far, going by car can still be faster. And once again: the more people are in the car, the cheaper it gets.

Host That makes sense. Now one last question: what about public transport?

Amanda Well, that's an even better way to get around, of course. CO_2 emissions are a lot lower when you take the bus or go by train. The only way to travel greener would be to go by bicycle or walking [sic, besser wäre *walk*]. That produces the lowest carbon footprint, which won't surprise you, but you're going to need pretty strong legs to do a 300-mile trip by foot or bike, right?

Host OK, thank you for answering Michael's question. Hope you got your answer, Michael. Next, we have another question for our expert Amanda Stokker. Rebecca from Burke wants to know ...

a)

One person in a car on a trip of 300 miles produces 104 kg CO_2.

Four people in a car on a trip of 300 miles produce 104 kg CO_2.

One person on a plane on a trip of 300 miles produces 184 kg CO_2.

Four people on a plane on a trip of 300 miles produce 736 kg CO_2.

b)

1 Many people prefer flying because it's cheaper and it saves time.

2 A longer trip by car can be cheaper than flying if there are more people in the car.

3 If you use public transport, emissions are a lot lower.

08 2 A family discussion

a)

Dad Oh can you pass me the sugar there Sarah.

Sarah Yeah, here you are. Could I have the milk, please?

Dad Yeah, yeah, OK.

Dad All right now, listen to this kids. I saw a leaflet. This is a car sharing scheme. It sounds really interesting. I don't know exactly what it costs but anyway, let me tell you the details.

Sarah So you, wait, do you mean we're gonna get rid of our car?

Dad No, no, this's, just wait a moment. So first of all, we don't have to own a car, OK, just become a member of this scheme and they run lots of cars. There's cars parked at different places all over the city. You just book a car on the internet, you know, and you can and drive if it's available.

Sarah How much is that gonna cost, Dad?

Dad Well, that's the thing I don't yet know, Sarah, but anyway, just listen to the details, cause it sounds very interesting. Now I had never thought about this before but I think it's really really interesting. I mean, first of all you help the environment. OK. And this, you know, I think we should all try to make a difference. And we don't drive that much in a whole year here anyway, ...

Sarah Yeah, but ...

Dad We're on a bike ... Wait a minute. This would save money, it's keeping people fit, and we can use public transport, it's cheaper, we haven't got to pay tax, or insurance for the car. Now, I don't know what it costs yet, that's true, OK, but I have been thinking of selling the family car so 'cause we don't really need a car.

Chris, Sarah But Dad!

→

Chris But Dad, we don't live in London, or any big city where we really have the opportunity to take public transportation or anything.

Sarah It's true!

Chris It's really difficult.

Sarah Having a car, that gives you freedom Dad, you know. And next year I'm gonna be 17 and I was really looking forward to start [sic, besser wäre *starting*] to learn to drive.

Dad Don't you think there's enough cars in the world, Sarah? Yeah, OK. But you haven't got to start, you haven't got to have a car straight away. – You can learn how to drive ... you're only 17.

Sarah Yeah, but, you know, if we have a car, then I can do lessons with you as well as with it, with an instructor and that's gonna save me a lot of money.

Dad Yes, I suppose you're right.

Sarah What about like, last week when I went to Rachel's party, and you picked me up at like midnight. Would you be able to do that with one of those car sharing cars?

Dad We can get a taxi if we need it.

Sarah Yeah, but ...

Dad There won't be a party every week.

Sarah Then what about the shopping? I don't wanna carry the shopping on my bike, Dad.

Chris No, honestly, what about our holidays?

Sarah Yeah, that's a good point.

Chris Are we gonna take the train or we're going to fly or ...

Sarah How do we get to the airport with all those suitcases?

Chris Are you going to pay for all those tickets, yeah? Exactly.

Dad Why do you need a car to do that?

Chris Because Sarah has like so much luggage with her all the time ...

Sarah I do not.

Chris Yes, you do.

Dad To take it on holiday?

Sarah No. You just making it up.

Dad Oh come on, just be realistic, think about it. I know you, you're, you're ... You were born in a different generation. You do really expect to have a car, a computer and all this other stuff, and I think a lot of it is not necessary or at least we could share things instead of everybody owning their own car, their own computer.

Chris I don't know about that ... I really don't know. But I did actually hear ... well, I did actually hear about something similar. But it doesn't require you to actually sell your own car. It's called something like, erm, rent your neighbour's car or using your neighbour's car or something like that. Let me just discuss this with you guys.

Sarah OK.

Chris This is the idea: you register online and, erm, basically you can just rent out your car to people who need it and they pay you know by the hour or however you want them to pay, and you set your own rates and you only ever have to pay, you know, pay the organization, mmh, whenever somebody uses the platform online to rent your car. But it doesn't require you to sell the car. So ...

Sarah So you've got the freedom of having your car.

Chris Yeah, exactly. Because I mean honestly as I said: as a family you do actually eventually need a car and if you don't have one and, you know, a situation occurs where you do need one desperately ...

Dad Well, have you got any more details about it?

Chris I don't know, I don't know where I read it, I don't know what it costs but I do actually, I read about it, it's for free, its online registration's free.

Dad Can you find the details?

Chris Yeah, I can just check online, and you just pay for it whenever somebody rents your car.

Sarah I think that sounds like a really good idea. Yeah, I think it's better than the whole car sharing scheme ...

Dad All right. Then shall we do that?

Sarah Yeah, let's look into it.

Dad OK, what about some breakfast?

Sarah Yes, cornflakes, please.

Chris Good idea.

Dad Thank God for that.

a)

1 Dad	a)	tells his kids that he is going to sell the family car.	
	b)	wants to make a difference and help the environment.	✔
	c)	wants to get fit.	
	d)	wants to go by bike.	

2 Sarah	a)	sees a problem with the shopping.	✔
	b)	is 17 years old.	
	c)	wants to take a taxi to get home after a party.	
	d)	wants to go on holiday by car.	

3 Sarah	a)	doesn't like Chris's idea.	
	b)	wants to have driving lessons with her father.	✔
	c)	wants her father to give her a car as a birthday present.	
	d)	worries that she cannot take all her suitcases with her when they go on holiday.	

4 Chris	a)	likes his father's idea.	
	b)	would like to use public transport.	
	c)	wants to go on holidays by plane.	
	d)	only has some information about another car sharing system.	✔

b)

Dad: 2, 4, 5, 9

Chris: 1, 3, 4, 6, 7, 8, 10

Lerntipp **Listening Skills üben**

- Höre dir englische Songs an und versuche, einzelne Wörter oder auch Sätze zu verstehen.
- Höre sie immer wieder an und erschließe dir so immer mehr Text.
- Wenn du das Gefühl hast, dass ein spezielles Wort, das du nicht verstehst, sehr wichtig ist, kannst du auch im Wörterbuch nachschlagen.

LANGUAGE

1 WORDS The environment

a)

Mögliche Lösungen:

carbon dioxide, carbon footprint, global warming, pollution, emission, insulation

b)

Mögliche Lösungen:

Many people try to reduce their carbon footprint.

Global warming is one of the problems we have to deal with.

Good insulation is important for all houses.

2 GRAMMAR REVISION + An old woman is talking about cars

I can remember the times when nobody in our village had a car. And I still remember the day when the first car drove down the main street in our village. That was around the year 1938. Everybody ran into the street when the car came nearer. It was an attraction for everybody. Our family didn't have a car until 1955. My sister and I were very proud when our father arrived in front of our house with the new family car.

Today it's different. Almost every family has a car, some even have two. But things change: there are people who don't want a car. They use public transport because it is cheaper and it helps the environment.

I sold my car ten years ago when I was 80. And I gave my driving licence to the town hall on the same day.

Today I take a taxi when I need to go somewhere.

3 GRAMMAR REVISION + A project for parents and young people

There was an interesting project at Seaview High School last weekend. The day was announced on the internet as a hands-on day for children and their parents.

The police wanted to inform the families about the dangers of the internet and how they can protect themselves.

A policeman talked about safety on the internet and gave many examples of what can be done. Parents and children were asked to tell the others about their experience with the internet.

A second very important topic was social networking sites because they are used by more and more teenagers. Children were asked what they do first when they come home after school. They answered that they communicated on social networking sites for more than half an hour.

"The internet gives you a lot of freedom but it also takes people's time," the policeman said.

During the workshop the parents had to do several tasks. Many of them were helped by their children.

At the end, everybody was invited to ask questions, and the policeman answered them patiently.

MEDIATION

1 An energy day

Mögliche Lösung:

Tim Was steht da eigentlich über die EUSEW?

Du Es ist eine Initiative der Europäischen Kommission in Brüssel. Sie besteht seit 2006. (3P)

Tim Können wir das auch hier bei uns in Sachsen machen oder geht das nur in Brüssel?

Du Das geht auch bei uns. (1P)

Tim Ist das nun eine Woche oder ein Tag, den wir organisieren sollen?

Du Es ist ein Tag. (1P)

Tim Und es muss genau in der Zeit vom 18.–22. Juni sein? Da haben wir doch unsere Parisfahrt.

Du Es ist auch an den Wochenenden davor und danach möglich. (1P)

Tim Also gut, ich stell mir vor, wir könnten da was mit unserem Fußballverein machen und uns nebenbei etwas für die Vereinskasse verdienen. Was meinst du?

Du Das geht leider nicht, es darf kein Verdienst gemacht werden. (1P)

Tim Was für einen Nutzen hätten wir dann für unseren Verein überhaupt?

Du Die Leute werden auf uns aufmerksam, vielleicht bekommen wir neue Mitglieder und es wird wahrscheinlich auch ein Zeitungsartikel erscheinen. (3P)

Tim Das ist natürlich auch gut. Und was müssen wir tun, wenn wir mitmachen wollen?

Du Wir müssen uns anmelden und dann können wir ihnen unsere Projektidee mitteilen, die wir an dem Tag realisieren wollen. (2P)

2 Get on your bike

Mögliche Lösung:

The government wants to double the number of bikes in cities and towns within the next ten years. (2P) The project is called “RadKultur”. (1P) They want more people to use their bikes and to make the bike more popular. (2P) A team of experts is going to make suggestions where to build more bike paths. (1P) The project will be realized in Tübingen, Lörrach and Mannheim first. (1P) They are thinking of competitions for good ideas and they want to have special activities at schools to make the bike more popular. (3P) Later they also want to have companies as their partner because they say that companies must learn to accept the bike too. (2P)

Lerntipp **Einen deutschen Text sinngemäß ins Englische übertragen**

Wenn du einen deutschen Text ins Englische übertragen sollst, musst du versuchen, dich von dem genauen Wortlaut der Sätze zu lösen. Deine Aufgabe besteht darin, den Sinn möglichst fehlerfrei auf Englisch wiederzugeben.
Weißt du ein bestimmtes Wort nicht, überlege, wie du den Satz anders ausdrücken kannst, ohne dass sich der Sinn ändert. Manchmal hilft es auch, den Satz ein wenig umzustellen.
Wenn du mit solchen Aufgaben noch Schwierigkeiten hast, kannst du immer wieder üben, kleine Äußerungen oder Sätze (z.B. aus der Zeitung) ins Englische zu übertragen. Benutze das Wörterbuch nur, wenn du gar nicht mehr weiter kommst.

WRITING

A car of your own?

Mögliche Lösung:

I have many friends who are thinking about having their own car. I am going to write about whether or not I would like to have a car of my own. (2P)

First, a car is very expensive. You have to buy petrol. You also have to pay a mechanic when your car is broken and you need somebody to repair it, for example. (3P)

Second, thinking of my carbon footprint, I do not think it is good to have a car because I will probably use my car alone very often. This is not good for the environment, and I think everybody should do something about pollution. (4P)

On the other hand, you can do car sharing with your friends. It is also comfortable to have a car because it is always in front of your house and you can also transport things easily. Going by car can save a lot of time. However, using public transport is sometimes even quicker than a car. (5P)

To sum up, I think that it is better for the environment to use public transport if you have the chance. I do not want to spend so much money on a car either. So this means I don't want a car of my own. (3P)

SPEAKING

09 How ecology-minded are we?

First let me describe the cartoon:

The cartoon shows a scene in a school. A girl and her teacher are standing in a classroom in front of the board. The teacher is an older woman who is looking surprised. She has some paper and a pen in her hands. The girl is smaller than the teacher and she is looking up to her. She has an open book in her hands and she is asking her teacher a question: “Explain to me again why our ecology textbook is printed on dead trees.” The teacher looks as if she doesn’t know the answer.

Second I’d like to say what the cartoon is about and what the message could be.

The cartoon is about saving the environment and stopping global warming. The girl is talking about her ecology book. The ecology book deals with environmental problems and I think in the ecology book you can find many suggestions what we can do to save the environment. And I can imagine that one of the tips is to save trees because trees use CO_2 and produce clean air.

Now the girl wants to know from the teacher why her ecology book is printed on ‘dead trees’ as trees were needed to produce the paper for the book, yet the message in the book is to save trees.

The girl might represent the younger generation who may be able to teach the older generation to think differently about how they can help to save the environment (e.g. no paper in classrooms, using computers rather than books etc.)

Now I’d like to talk about my opinion:

I like the cartoon because it makes clear that very often it’s easy to give tips about how to save the environment but it’s difficult to carry out this advice in real life.

I think we all need books but on the other hand we should try to save paper. I think we can save paper if we think before printing things from the computer.

Now you

Mögliche Lösung:

Let me describe the cartoon first:

The cartoon shows a scene in a shoe shop. A man is sitting there and trying on shoes. The shop assistant is sitting on the floor and showing him different shoes. He has one shoe in his hand and explains to the customer: "We have a new line of environmentally-friendly shoes. They leave a low carbon footprint." The customer is older than the shop assistant. He's wearing a tie and looks like a business man. He looks as if he doesn't understand the shop assistant's message. (7P)

Second I'd like to say what the cartoon is about and what the message could be:

The cartoon is about keeping our carbon footprint low. I think it wants to show that sometimes things are sold with a special message. In this case, the message wants to make the man think that he is doing something for the environment when he buys the shoes. The message could also be that you can keep your carbon footprint low when you buy something special which may be a bit more expensive. In fact your carbon footprint is still high, of course, but with the new thing you can feel better if you think of your carbon footprint. (6P)

In my opinion, this cartoon is really good. Of course, everybody knows that you can't keep your carbon footprint low with a pair of shoes. This message makes me laugh. But everybody should pay attention when he or she buys something. The message is not to believe that you can buy something and the result is that your carbon footprint is low. No, you must become active yourself. (5P)

My family and I try to save energy whenever we can. When leaving a room, we always turn off the lights. And we leave the car in the garage whenever it makes sense. (2P)

LISTENING

10 Great success for students

Reporter Hello everybody out there. This is Ben on "Radio for friends". I'm here at Midland School today. Maybe you've heard about the huge problems students have been having recently with public transport. For those of you who don't know: every March and October the city's bus timetables are changed. So far the changes have been small and haven't really affected the students.
But this year was very different. The changes meant that students from the northern areas of the city had to wait nearly an hour for their bus home. As we heard on the nine o'clock news, the bus company has since decided to change the [time] tables again following huge protests from [sic; besser wäre *by*] students, teachers and parents from the school. So, let's find out just how they stood up for their rights!
I have Steve with me here. Hi, Steve, tell me how the timetable changes affected you.

Steve Oh, yeah, well, I live in the north, about 7 miles away from school. I used to catch bus number 13 at 4.05 after school. And I'd get home around 4.40 every day. But with the new timetable, you know, I had to wait until 4.50 and got home at 5.27. The worst thing was that the school closes at 4 and I always had to wait outside. Nobody else had to wait as long as I did and I couldn't do anything the whole time, not even homework or anything. Well, I could listen to music, but that was it. And when I got home, it was already dinner time and then I had to do my homework afterwards. So, like, there was no time for hanging out with friends or playing football or anything. It was really bad, so I'm pretty pleased that they've changed the timetable.

Reporter Oh, yes, I can believe you. It must have been terrible. So, now Melissa, hi! What's been your experience?

Melissa Hi. Yeah, umm, I also live in the north and I usually catch bus number 28 to go to school. When the timetable changed, I had to get up 45 minutes earlier. And I had to walk to a different bus stop which was so far away. And I got home 35 minutes later in the evening. That adds up to a lot of time every day! It was bad for getting my homework done and because I never had time to play tennis anymore. And the worst thing was that I had to wait in school for ages every morning before lessons began. It was a complete waste of time! I pay a lot of money for my bus ticket and I think I have the right to get to school at an acceptable time. I couldn't believe that the bus company changed the timetable just to save money or something like that. So, yeah, so then a few of us decided to do something about the situation.

Reporter Yes, and you've been successful. We'll be hearing about that in a minute when I talk to one of your teachers, Mr Burton. I can really understand that you're angry, though.
Thanks, Melissa. Speak to you later.

a)

Mögliche Lösungen:

1 Name the months when timetables change.	March and October
2 Give information about the experience with the timetable changes so far. *(2 facts)*	small and haven't really affected the student
3 Say when the listeners found out that the bus company had reacted to the protests?	in the news at nine
4 Give reasons why the bus company reacted.	protest of students, letter to newspapers, students talked to the manager
5 Give two facts about where Steve lives.	in the north, 7 miles away from school
6 Name three reasons why the new timetable was bad for Steve.	1 had to wait until 4.50 2 had to wait outside school 3 couldn't meet his friends anymore
7 Name three ways the new timetable affected Melissa.	1 had to get up 45 minutes earlier 2 had to walk further to the bus stop 3 got home 35 minutes later
8 Explain why Melissa thought that the bus company's timetable changes were not OK.	she pays a lot of money for her ticket

11 *Reporter* Welcome back. With me is Mr Burton, a teacher at the school. Mr Burton, what did you do with your students in class to react against the changes to the bus timetables?

Mr Burton Hello, yes, umm ... it's very important for our school to teach the students the ideas behind democracy. We try to run the school democratically too and we allow our students to have their say by encouraging them to talk about any issues or problems in class. These discussions often become quite lively debates. With the bus timetable situation, it was very interesting to see that it wasn't just one or two students who complained about the changes but almost the whole class had something to say. We tried to think about what we could do and talked about how we might be able to change the bus company's decision. And after a long discussion we agreed on different things:

The first was that the students wanted to write a letter to local newspapers and inform them about the situation. Then they planned to go and talk to the manager of the bus service. And finally they decided to go into town and tell people on the streets about it all, so they created colourful posters.

Reporter OK, all those sound like good plans. And how did they get on?

Mr Burton Well, there was a huge response to their activities: a lot of people answered their letter in the newspaper. And nearly all of them agreed that the timetable changes were unfair. The manager really listened to what the students had to say. I think he was quite impressed by their attitude. And on that single Saturday morning in town, they managed to collect 388 signatures against the change to the timetables.

I think that the activities were a positive thing because they made the students realize how important it is to have their say. At the time, they didn't know if they'd be successful or not. But they were, and the bus times have been changed back again. I feel that the whole situation was very important for them to experience how getting involved and fighting for your rights can lead to success. Even if it does mean hard work. And for myself, I have to say: I'm so proud of them, they did a really good job!

Reporter Oh yes, I'd agree with that. Thank you Mr Burton. It was great to hear such a fantastic success story!

Now we have a mother on the phone. Hi Mrs Miller. So, what did you like about this protest?

→

Mrs Miller Hi. Yes, well, I very much liked the way the whole process worked. I was surprised at how quickly the students reacted. I think it's brilliant that the school and the teachers give them room to discuss things like that in class. The teachers were so ready to help the students, which was great. But what really impressed me was that even though the bus timetable changes hadn't affected all the students negatively, many students still stood up and had their say. They supported their classmates. I think that showed that the school is doing a great job of teaching the kids how democracy works.

I also liked the way they tried to put the public in the picture. The students talked to people in their free time, you know, they tried to get them to support their protest and they asked for signatures. And, luckily, they were really polite and everything went off very peacefully. There was no vandalism or anything like that. I think it all went very well. And I'm happy that the bus times have been changed again!

Reporter Yeah, you have a child who was very much affected by the changes, don't you?

Mrs Miller Haha, yes I do.

Reporter Well, it looks like the students' hard work has paid off! What a great result. Thanks for coming on the show, Mrs Miller, and I hope Melissa enjoys getting up a bit later again! So, next we're going to play you some music …

b)

Mögliche Lösungen:

1 teachers encourage their students to talk about their problems

2 wrote an open letter to the newspaper, went and talked to the manager of the bus company, informed people in the streets, created posters

3 people answered the open letter, the manager of the bus company listened to the students, the students got 388 signatures

4 the students could see that it is important to have your say

5 how quickly the students reacted, teachers were ready to help, students supported their classmates, no vandalism

LANGUAGE

1 WORDS Creating new words

a)

1	true	truth
2	poor	poverty
3	(to) think	thought
4	(to) annoy	annoying
5	sense	sensitive, sensible
6	(to) apologize	apology
7	(to) feel	feeling
8	(to) speak	speech
9	concentration	(to) concentrate
10	(to) immigrate	immigration, immigrant

b)

1 The poverty of some London families is so alarming that the London authority wants to help them.

2 I like Sam's new girlfriend. But yesterday she didn't tell the truth when we talked about her last job.

3 Last month the Mayor of London talked to the public about his future plans. His speech was fantastic.

4 My boyfriend really hurt me last week. Now I'm waiting for his apology.

c)

Mögliche Lösungen:

1 What do you think? Tell me your thoughts on this topic.

2 It's really annoying that Paul is always late for work.

2 GRAMMAR REVISION + A discussion about bus times

Before the campaign

1 I will have to catch the early bus at 7.10 if I want to be at school on time.

2 If the bus company doesn't change the times, we will go on strike.

3 I won't be able to take part in the dancing lessons any more if I don't get home until 5.20 pm.

During the campaign

1 If we talked to the bus company, perhaps they would change the times again.

2 We could inform a lot of people in town if we went to the market square on Saturday morning.

3 If we collected a lot of signatures from people in town, we could give them to the bus company.

After the campaign

1 If all the students had accepted the new bus times, some of them wouldn't have had time for hobbies after school.

2 If the students hadn't written the letter to the newspaper, the public wouldn't have known about the issue.

3 If the students hadn't done such a good job, the bus company wouldn't have reacted.

Lerntipp if-Sätze

- Sieh dir die drei Sätze vom Handhinweis vor der Aufgabe nochmals an und schreibe sie in dein Lernheft.
- Schreibe unter jede Verbform den Namen der Zeit. So erkennst du, wie die Zeiten in den drei Arten von if-Sätzen verwendet werden.
- Bist du noch unsicher, dann sieh im Grammar File 9 auf S. 163 in deinem Englischbuch nach.

3 GRAMMAR Teens speak out

Students had the chance to discuss problem issues

"Teens Speak Out" began last Saturday morning with a short speech and an explanation of Rule No. 1: "You adults out there aren't allowed to speak now," presenter Phil Cross told the audience.
During the discussion, students shared their opinions about many different topics. They spoke about communication with teachers and the head teacher, the importance of sports and about school safety.
14-year-old student Alan said that it was necessary to improve contact with the head teacher. "The only time you hear from the head teacher is during an assembly, or when she's addressing all the students, or when there's something going on that she doesn't like," he said.
Sue, aged 15, agreed. She wanted the head teacher to see and recognize the good work that is done by many students. "It's time the head teacher changed something. At the moment she only speaks to us when something is going wrong. Things would be much better if she saw the good work and talked to the students about their success."

4 GRAMMAR REVISION + Word order

1 Last week we had a great meeting. / We had a great meeting last week.
2 First of all, we took a picture for the School Yearbook.
3 Then there was a long discussion about the school shop.
4 Nearly all the students enjoy buying things at the shop.
5 We heard what they like and what needs to be improved.
6 After that we talked about the youth club. / We talked about the youth club after that.
7 Unfortunately, we didn't have time to finish the discussion.
8 So we are going to meet again next Saturday.

5 Everyday English: Solving conflicts

Mögliche Lösungen:

You ▶ start the conversation	*Excuse me, Anna, can I have a word with you?*
You ▶ name the problem	As you can see, I'd like to cook my dinner but I can't because the kitchen is in an awful mess. I think you used the kitchen just before me. (2P)
Anna ▶ disagree that there is a problem and start talking about how wonderful your dinner was	Yes, that's right. But where's the problem? It isn't in such a mess. I also had to clean up the kitchen because the last person had not done it. And I had such wonderful spaghetti, it was great! Oh I love spaghetti. Do you like spaghetti with tomato sauce too? (4P)
You ▶ explain the problem again	Yes, I do. But the problem is that you left the kitchen so dirty that I can't cook. I don't want to clean up your mess. That's the problem. (3P)
Anna ▶ apologize, find a way to solve the problem	I'm sorry. I should have cleaned the kitchen. I'll do it right away. Is that OK? (3P)
You ▶ accept the apology and make a suggestion	It's OK for me. And I'll help you. And maybe we can agree to clean the kitchen after we use it? (3P)
Anna ▶ accept the suggestion	OK, that's a good idea and very nice of you, thank you. (2P)

WRITING

1 Young people and their attitude towards the internet

Mögliche Lösung:

The internet has become very popular in the last few years, especially with young people. (1P)

However, there are teenagers who see the internet critically. Some say it is not safe because their personal information might be misused. Another argument is that surfing the internet costs too much and also takes too much time which could be used for other things, e.g. volunteering to help others. (4P)

I surf the internet almost every day. I communicate with my friends on social networking sites and I use it for collecting information. (3P)

I do not agree with most of the critical statements. Communicating with your friends is important and can be very quick on the internet. And, for example, if you need information for a presentation, surfing the internet is a lot quicker than going to the library. We have a flat rate, so it is not expensive. (4P)

Of course, everybody should be careful with the personal information they put on the internet. This can be very dangerous. (1P)

To sum up, I would say that young people need the internet to lead a modern life. The internet is great for communication and for information. (2P)

Lerntipp So kannst du beim Writing besser werden:

- Ein ganz wichtiger Schritt, um beim **Writing** besser zu werden, ist die Überprüfung deines Textes. So kannst du feststellen, an welchen Stellen du deinen Text nochmal überarbeiten kannst und worauf du beim nächsten Mal besonders achten solltest.

Überprüfe wichtige Punkte anhand der folgenden Liste.

- Du kannst diese Liste immer wieder verwenden.
- Unten hast du Gelegenheit, eigene Punkte einzufügen, auf die du in Zukunft besonders achten willst.

• Brief / E-Mail: Anrede, Grußformel? • Bericht / Geschichte / Diskussion: Überschrift?		
• Aufgabenstellung genau beachtet?		
• Einleitung / einleitender Satz am Anfang?		
• Text durch Absätze logisch strukturiert?		
• Unterschiedliche Satzstrukturen (z.B. Relativsätze, Sätze mit **linking words**) verwendet?		
• Rechtschreibung und Grammatik (Zeiten, Wortstellung) okay?		
• Sinnvolle Länge der Sätze?		
• Brief / E-Mail: Schlussformel? • Bericht / Geschichte / Diskussion: Schlusssatz?		
•		
•		
•		

2 A letter to the newspaper about a youth club

Mögliche Lösung:

Dear Sir or Madam, (1P)

I am an exchange student from Germany. At the moment I am staying here in Bristol. (2P)

I am very interested in the discussion about the new youth club because in Germany I am a member of a youth club team. (2P)

We have a programme of many different activities, e.g. skateboarding, music evenings, computer lessons and games for all ages. (2P)

There was a time when we had a problem with alcohol, but our social worker invited us to talk openly about our experience. This helped and now it is OK again. (3P)

I can only recommend a youth club for Bristol: it will help young people a lot because many teenagers will find a place where they can meet new friends and take part in the many activities offered. (3P)

I hope that the youth club will open soon and I am looking forward to visiting it. (2P)

Yours faithfully, (1P)

…

Lösungen B

READING

Report on young Londoners

a)

Mögliche Lösungen:

1 What were four of the topics of the survey?	education, safety, transport, getting involved
2 Who was interviewed *(2 facts)*?	more than 1000 Londoners aged 11–16
3 Why did they need the 2004 survey?	to compare 2009 results with 2004.

b)

1 When talking about living in London, shopping	a) is the most important thing for young Londoners.	
	b) only comes second.	✔
	c) is not mentioned.	
2 The 2009 survey shows that	a) most young Londoners have tried to change something in their area.	✔
	b) it's necessary to activate more young people.	
	c) many young people think you can't change anything by getting involved.	
3 If you compare the results of 2004 and 2009,	a) in 2004, fewer young people said that they could take part in decisions at schools.	✔
	b) more people felt safe in 2004.	
	c) issues about the environment were not a problem in 2009.	
4 When talking about safety and crime,	a) many young people say that they have been victim to violent crime.	
	b) teenagers hanging around is one of the biggest problems.	
	c) many young Londoners would like the police to be more present in London.	✔
5 The survey says that	a) most young people walk to school although they could use the bus for free.	
	b) young Londoners don't walk because of the Zip Card.	
	c) the bus is the favourite form of transport.	✔
6 When talking about the environment,	a) young Londoners make it clear that parks are very important.	✔
	b) waste and air quality are the most important issues.	
	c) more young people mentioned the pollution of the waterways as a problem than rubbish.	
7 Many young people think	a) that the quality of their schools could be better.	
	b) that they will find a job in the London area.	✔
	c) that London cannot provide good opportunities in difficult times.	

LANGUAGE

1 WORDS Have your say – a discussion

The next public discussion on important local topics will be held on Wednesday, 7 July at 7.30 pm. This time the discussion will be on the mosquito device which has been installed in front of the youth club. As usual, interesting guests will take part and discuss the topic, for example Mr Pit Hank, a politician here in our town. Mr Hank thinks the mosquito device is a useful thing and that it makes sense where it is. Then there are Tom and Nicholas, two students who have started a petition. Tom and Nicholas don't want to accept the mosquito device in front of the youth club any longer. And there is Mrs Felder. Although Mrs Felder lives near the youth club, she supports the campaign against the mosquito device. Also there will be Mr Jeff Saltman who says that the mosquito device can't be removed unless the young people get a new place to meet. Peter Smith, the well-known presenter from Radio Young, will lead the discussion.
Place: Grattan's Hotel 24, Swansea Road.

2 WORDS Students talking in a school break

1 I think Jo is very good at presenting topics.
2 I'm afraid of failing our Maths test tomorrow.
3 Mrs Sutter is a really good teacher. Her attitude towards the students is excellent.
4 I can't blame anybody else for my bad mark in English – I have just been too lazy the last few months.
5 I'm glad that Sue apologized to me for her bad behaviour.
6 I read in the school magazine that the number of hours spent on homework at our school has risen by ten per cent in the last two years.
7 I don't think that Mr Gardener is prejudiced against any of the students, he's very fair.
8 John is really interested in German history, he knows so much!
9 Mark will throw a big party on Friday evening.
10 Did you know that Mrs Sutter is married to a Swiss man?

3 WORDS Explaining words

Mögliche Lösungen:

1 fare	It's something/the amount of money you must pay before you go by train or bus or underground.
2 (to) tell the truth	It's the opposite of 'to tell lies'.
3 equal	Men and women have equal rights. This means that they are allowed to do the same things.
4 (to) immigrate	When you immigrate to a country, you go to that country to live there.
5 (to) complain	If you are in a restaurant and the food is bad, you can complain to the chef.
6 tax	Tax is the money you pay to the government.
7 likely	It's a synonym for 'probably'.

4 GRAMMAR REVISION + About Ann's presentation

a)

1 I think she was a bit nervous.

2 She had prepared her presentation well.

3 Ann talked in a way that I could follow her presentation easily.

4 Personally, I liked the way she kept looking at the audience.

5 The outline was worked out carefully.

6 The photos she showed were fantastic.

b)

Mögliche Lösungen:

1 The presentation was great/interesting/bad/boring. (adjective)

2 She talked too quietly/loudly/slowly/quickly/fast. (adverb)

3 I think people liked listening because the topic was so interesting/exciting. (adjective)

5 GRAMMAR REVISION + Talking about the future

a)

1 Look, here is the ticket for my flight. I'm flying to Spain tomorrow.

2 Lisa has just given me a call. I think she'll be late for dinner.

3 I'm sorry, mum. I haven't had time to tidy up my room. I'll do it after school. I promise!

4 Nick's just told me about his problems at school. We're going to talk to the teachers in a few days.

5 It's terribly cold, isn't it? But it'll be warmer next week.

6 It's Sue's birthday in a few days. I'm going to send her a nice birthday card.

7 We've already booked our holidays for next year. We're going to Florida again.

8 This year Susanna was chosen to play the main part in the school theatre production. I'm sure that next year it'll be you, Alice.

b)

Mögliche Lösungen:

1 I'm going to talk to my teacher tomorrow.

2 I think John will be our coach next year.

3 I'm meeting friends this evening.

MEDIATION

Have your say on Highway 2A

Mögliche Lösungen:

1 Die Verkehrsbehörde erstellt derzeit einen Bericht über die Sicherheit auf dem Highway 2A. Die Gemeinde soll auch ihre Meinung abgeben und wurde zum Workshop eingeladen. (3P)

2 Sie werden über die Gefahren des Highway 2A befragt. (1P)

3 Das Treffen findet in Form eines Workshops statt. (1P)

4 Die Bürger müssen sich registrieren. (1P)

5 Die Bürger können sich auch online oder via E-Mail beteiligen. (2P)

6 Es wurden Mitteilungen an die Haushalte verteilt, die auf den Workshop hingewiesen haben. Sie enthielten auch die Telefonnummer, unter der man sich registrieren kann. (3P)

SPEAKING

12 At the end of school

Hi, my name's Paul, and I'm talking about my experiences at Mittelberg Realschule today. I've been at this school for six years now. I'm going to divide my talk into 4 parts. First, I'm going to talk about the first couple of years. Then I'm going to talk about years 7 and 8, then about years 9 and 10. I'll end my talk with a little summary.

When I first started at this school, I was 10 years old. I was really worried about the school, new teachers, new classmates and of course about the new subjects. I didn't know what it was going to be like. But very soon I found a good friend who I did everything with. And our teachers were really helpful trying to settle us into the new situation. They didn't just try to help us with our learning, but lots of them also listened to our problems and tried to find ways to solve them. So after a few months everything was OK. My worries were gone and I felt OK at the new school.

Now, years 7 and 8. Those were pretty hard years, I have to say. To be honest, school definitely wasn't my favourite thing at that time. I didn't work enough at home or at school, so my marks got bad and I got lazier and lazier. You probably know the situation, right? It's very difficult to get out of it. So I didn't want to go to school any more. But my parents kept telling me it was the right thing to stay and I would miss so many opportunities if I left. So in the end, I stayed.

This leads me to years 9 and 10 now. They were better. My teachers encouraged me to start thinking about what I wanted to do after school – like which job would be good for me, what I wanted to do with my life and all that. I realized that I had to work harder at school if I wanted to get a job I'm interested in. So, I needed good marks at the end of year 10. That thought made me work harder, really hard sometimes. And it worked! My marks got better and now I have a good report, and I hope it will be enough to become a computer engineer.

To sum up my talk about my years at school, I have to say I've had quite a good time here. I could have done with more help in years 7 and 8 because they were really hard. But I somehow got through them, I just kept going and tried my best. Maybe some careers advice would have been good, it might have helped me to see what I wanted to do later on. But, anyway, I could make without it! I think Mittelberg Realschule is a good school with good teachers. And I'd be really happy if my talk helps you to think positively if you ever have a few problems at some point at school. Remember: never give up!

Thank you very much.

Now you

Mögliche Lösung:

Hello, my name is Laura and I would like to talk about the last six years at this school. I'm going to subdivide my talk into four parts. First, I'm going to talk about my first two years here. Then I would like to say something about years 7 and 8, then about 9 and 10. To finish my talk, I will give you a short summary. (2P)

When I first came here, I was very nervous and very sad. On the one hand, I was happy because my best friend Rebecca also came to this school. On the other hand, I missed my other friends. I could only meet them after school. (2P) I have to say that I had problems here at first. My marks were not very good, and I had difficulties following the lessons. (1P) Some other students in my class were very good, and often they had already done what was new for me when I came here. (1P) But Rebecca and I started to learn together, that was very good. (1P) Our teachers were also friendly – and some of them were very strict! But after a while it became easier for me. (1P)

Now I come to years 7 and 8. They were fun! We went on a class trip, and I got to know many people from my class much better. That also made our lessons easier, and school suddenly became a place I wanted to go to. (2P) Well, I have to say that it was more because of the other students, not really because of the lessons! But the lessons were also OK and the teachers were always there to help us. (2P) Rebecca and I still had our learning group and others joined us, so we had a lot of fun working together. But our marks – yes, well, they didn't get better. But anyway, those years were great! (1P)

Now let me talk about years 9 and 10. They were much harder. My parents wanted me to get good marks at school because they wanted me to have a good job. (2P) This was difficult. My marks were always OK, not very good but OK, I was happy with them, and friends were more important to me anyway. (1P) But then I had to learn very hard, and my parents always wanted to see my homework and all that. This wasn't really fun anymore. But, yes, I have to say that they were right when they wanted me to become better. My marks became really good, and now I'm going to do an apprenticeship as a dentist's assistant. I hope I will like it! (2P)

To sum up my talk, I have to say that it was really fun being here. The teachers are helpful, and the students are very cool! You can have so much fun here! You also have many opportunities at this school and you can ask the teachers to help you. (2P)

I hope I was able to give you a good idea about my school life. Thank you very much. (1P)